Speedboats

Aaron Sautter
AR B.L.: 2.9
Points: 0.5

MG

HORSEPOWER

SPEEDBOATS

by Aaron Sautter

Reading Consultant:
Barbara J. Fox
Reading Specialist
North Carolina State University

Content Consultant:
Mark V. Wheeler
Board of Directors and Co-Chair, Junior Racing Division
American Power Boat Association

Capstone
press

Mankato, Minnesota

Blazers is published by Capstone Press,
151 Good Counsel Drive, P.O. Box 669, Mankato, Minnesota 56002.
www.capstonepress.com

Library of Congress Cataloging-in-Publication Data
Sautter, Aaron.
    Speedboats / by Aaron Sautter.
    p. cm.—(Blazers. Horsepower)
    Summary: "Discusses speedboats, their main features, and their
uses"—Provided by publisher.
    Includes bibliographical references and index.
    ISBN-13: 978-0-7368-6783-2 (hardcover)
    ISBN-10: 0-7368-6783-X (hardcover)
    1. Motorboats—Juvenile literature. 2. Motorboat racing—Juvenile
literature. I. Title. II. Series.
VM341.S279 2007
623.82'31—dc22   2006020961

Editorial Credits
Jenny Marks, editor; Patrick D. Dentinger, book designer; Jason Knudson,
    set designer; Jo Miller, photo researcher/photo editor

Photo Credits
Art Directors/Gary Kufner, 12–13, 15; Jim Ringland, 25; John Farmar, 11
Corbis/Bill Schild, 26–27; James L. Amos, 20
Getty Images Inc./AFP/Andy Newman, 8, 9; Florida Keys News Bureau/Andy
    Newman, 5, 7, 16–17; Sandra Mu, cover, 6; Stone/Oli Tennent, 28–29
Photo Courtesy of Mercury Racing, 19
PhotoEdit Inc./Jeff Greenberg, 22; Tom McCarthy, 23
Shutterstock/Zdorov Kirill Vladimirovich, 14
SuperStock/Mike Fuller Group, 21

1 2 3 4 5 6 12 11 10 09 08 07

TABLE OF CONTENTS

RACING ON THE WAVES

The crowd cheers as powerful engines roar to life. A horn sounds, and sleek speedboats blast through the water. The race is on!

The racers streak across the water.
Engines scream as the boats fly around
a sharp turn. In a spray of water, one
driver flips over into the waves.

BLAZER FACT

Speedboats rise up out of the water at high speeds. Boats travel faster when part of the hull is in the air.

Three boats are neck and neck. Each boat races for the lead. In a final burst of speed, the winner flashes past the finish line. Time to celebrate the win!

BLAZER FACT

Key West, Florida, is a hot spot for speedboat races. The Offshore World Championship rocks the harbor every year.

DESIGN

Speedboats come in different shapes and sizes. But they all have one thing in common—they're fast.

One or more large engines
power speedboats. The engines spin
propellers that push the boats up to
150 miles per hour (241 kph).

Monohull

Monohull speedboats have smooth,
V-shaped bodies. Catamaran speedboats
have two side-by-side hulls. Air flows
between the hulls and lifts catamarans
higher out of the water.

BLAZER FACT

Catamarans work best on smooth water, while monohulls work best in rough water.

Catamaran

Bright paint

Engine

Propeller

Cockpit

Hull

CRUISING IN STYLE

Speedboats offer more than speed and power. Boat owners ride the waves in style. Bright paint and sparkling decals give speedboats a flashy look.

Some speedboats are all about comfort. Decked-out cabins have mini kitchens, leather furniture, and even plasma TVs.

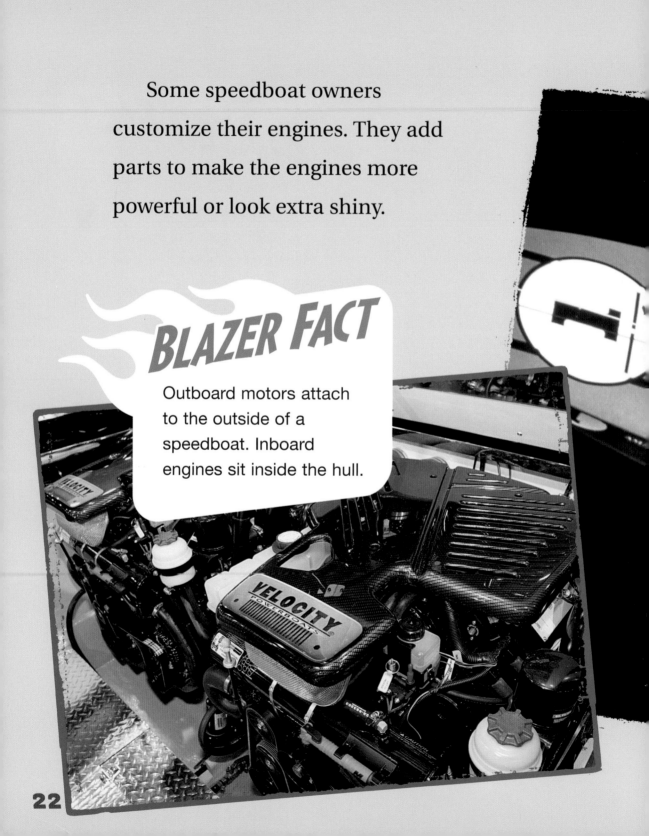

Some speedboat owners customize their engines. They add parts to make the engines more powerful or look extra shiny.

BLAZER FACT

Outboard motors attach to the outside of a speedboat. Inboard engines sit inside the hull.

SPEEDBOATS IN ACTION

Riding at high speeds is fun but dangerous. Racers wear helmets, life jackets, and other safety gear in case of crashes.

SWORLD SATELLITE 0947 880019
C51
RYA
REDDISH MARINE
Worries
A70

Whether racing across the ocean or just cruising the shoreline, speedboats always arrive with speed and style!

BLAZER FACT

Each year, owners show off their speedboats at the New York City Powerboat Rally on the Hudson River.

MAKING WAVES!

GLOSSARY

cabin (KAB-in)—a section of a boat where passengers or crew rest and relax

catamaran (KAT-uh-muh-ran)—a boat with two side-by-side hulls

customize (KUHSS-tuh-mize)—to change a vehicle according to the owner's needs and tastes

decal (DEE-kal)—a picture or label that can be transferred to hard surfaces

decked-out (DEKT-OUT)—filled with stylish, expensive products

hull (HUHL)—the main body of a boat

life jacket (LIFE JAK-it)—a device to keep you afloat if you fall in the water

monohull (MON-uh-huhl)—a boat with a single V-shaped hull

propeller (pruh-PEL-ur)—a rotating blade that moves a vehicle through water or air

READ MORE

Bullard, Lisa. *Powerboats.* Pull Ahead Books. Minneapolis: Lerner, 2004.

Dieker, Wendy Strobel. *Hydroplanes.* Horsepower. Mankato, Minn.: Capstone Press, 2007.

Morris, Mark. *Boats.* Mean Machines. Chicago: Raintree, 2005.

INTERNET SITES

FactHound offers a safe, fun way to find Internet sites related to this book. All of the sites on FactHound have been researched by our staff.

Here's how:
1. Visit *www.facthound.com*
2. Choose your grade level.
3. Type in this book ID **073686783X** for age-appropriate sites. You may also browse subjects by clicking on letters, or by clicking on pictures and words.
4. Click on the **Fetch It** button.

FactHound will fetch the best sites for you!

INDEX